THE WINTER OLYMPICS

G000038876

Contents

Written by Andy Seed

Collins

289074

Cornwall E.L.S.

The Winter Olympics

The Olympic Games is a huge sports competition that takes place every four years. Athletes from countries around the world compete to win medals in different events.

In the early days of the Summer Olympics, some winter sports, such as ice skating and ice hockey, were included. They had to be held months before the other events, when the weather was cold. Then, in the 1920s, the organisers decided to have a separate Winter Games when there would be more snow and ice.

2

The Winter Olympics are always held in a country where there is a lot of snow and ice. These countries are called host nations.

Canada

Norway

Germany

Austria

Yugoslavia

France

Russia

United States of America

Italy

Switzerland

Japan

PAST FACT

The United States has hosted the Winter Olympics four times – more than any other country.

On this map, host nations are shown in dark green.

The first Winter Olympics were held in 1924. These Games took place in the town of Chamonix in France. There were nine events and most of the 258 athletes were men.

The Winter Games became very popular. More countries and more people competed each time they were held.

Canada beat the United States in the ice hockey final at the 1924 Winter Olympics.

4

It isn't just the size of the Winter Olympics that has changed over time. In the early days, competitors wore heavy clothes made from wool and fur to keep them warm. Today, athletes wear very light **human-made fabrics**. These allow them to move quickly and easily.

The equipment used in the Winter Olympics has changed a lot over the years. It is now much safer and gives better results than in the early days.

the British curling team in 1924

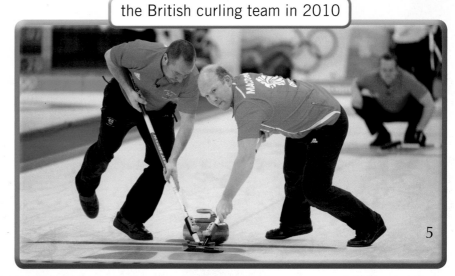

the British curling team in 2010

5

Figure skating is the oldest event in
the Winter Olympics. Pairs or single skaters
perform daring moves on the ice such
as spins, jumps and lifts.

SKATER TO FILM STAR

Sonja Henie from Norway
won the gold medal at three
different Olympic Games.
She was only 11 when she
first competed in 1924 –
the youngest ever Olympic
skater. Later, Sonja
became a film star.

Sonja in 1928

A team of judges awards scores to decide the winners in each event. Skaters can lose marks if a piece of their costume falls off!

Figure skating is the only Olympic event performed to music. In pairs, the skaters must keep in perfect time with each other to win top marks.

American skaters take part in the pairs figure skating at the 2010 Winter Olympics

The team sport of ice hockey was once part of the Summer Olympics but was moved to the Winter Games to stop the ice it was played on from melting.

Ice hockey was invented in Canada. Canada won gold medals at the first four Winter Olympics.

Ice hockey equipment

Ice hockey is now an indoor sport with lots of **physical** contact. Players barge into each other and the sticks used are hard, so everyone playing wears protective clothing.

FAST FACT

During a hockey game, the **puck** can reach a speed of over 160 kilometres an hour!

helmet

shoulder pads

gloves

hockey stick

padded stockings

skates

puck

9

Ski jumping  1924

Ski jumping is one of the most dramatic sports at the Winter Olympics.
Competitors ski down a steep ramp, then take off and jump as far as
possible down a long hill.

Ski jumpers must have great balance. Judges give points for each jump and award extra points for **style** and distance.

Ski jumping distances have increased as equipment and skills have improved. In 1808 the furthest distance was 9.5 metres, but in 2011 the record was 246 metres!

PAST FACT

The bronze medal for ski jumping at the first Winter Olympics was awarded to American Anders Haugen – 50 years after the event! A mistake in the scores was discovered by a historian. Anders was 86 years old when he received his medal in 1974.

Ski jumpers now use special long skis and hold them in a V-shape. These light skis are made from a very strong **plastic** called fibreglass.

11

A bobsleigh is a very fast sledge that runs along a track covered in ice. Competitors push the bobsleigh to start and then jump in.

The bobsleigh started out as a four-man event in 1924. Over the years, other races were added, including a 2-man race in 1932 and a 2-woman race in 2002.

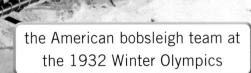

the American bobsleigh team at the 1932 Winter Olympics

A bobsleigh has no engine but it is faster than most trains. It can reach speeds of 120 kilometres an hour.

The bobsleigh is one of the most dangerous Olympic events. Crashes happen sometimes and the athletes can be seriously hurt or even killed.

PAST FACT

In 1988, the first ever team from a tropical country entered the bobsleigh event. The Jamaican team crashed, but they didn't give up. They walked with their bobsleigh down the track to cross the finish line!

the four-man bobsleigh event at the 2010 Winter Olympics

13

Downhill skiing is one of the fastest events at the Winter Olympics. Skiers race down a steep mountain course, which has lots of twists and turns.

The event came into the Games in 1936 because fast downhill ski races had become very popular.

The women's alpine skiing combined event at the 1936 Winter Olympics

14

FAST FACT

Skiers can reach speeds of up to 150 kilometres an hour on some parts of the downhill course!

Huge crowds enjoy watching Olympic skiing.

15

Downhill skiers need a lot of special equipment to keep them safe.

helmet

goggles

ski poles

one-piece ski suit

long skis

Athlete profile: Lindsey Vonn

Sport:	Skiing (all race events)
Country:	USA
Olympic medals:	Gold in 2010 women's downhill
Fact:	She won a cow for winning a ski race in France

Lindsey Vonn in the women's downhill skiing super-G race at the 2010 Winter Olympics

17

The Winter Paralympics are held after the Winter Olympics, in the same city. These Games are for athletes with disabilities, such as those who are blind or use a wheelchair. The Paralympics began when injured soldiers were helped to play sport after World War II. The first Winter Paralympics took place in Sweden in 1976.

There are six sports in the Winter Paralympics. Each sport is adapted for athletes with different disabilities.

Alpine skiing and Para-snowboarding

Skiers or snowboarders stand, sit or follow the voice of a guide to compete in different skiing events.

Ice sledge hockey

Athletes play using special sledges and two sticks.

18

Biathlon

Competitors ski along a course and stop at intervals to fire a **rifle** at targets.

Cross-country skiing

Blind or partly blind skiers are guided through the cross-country course by a sighted skier.

Wheelchair curling

Competitors in wheelchairs slide heavy stones across ice towards a target.

19

Special skiing equipment

Wheelchair athletes who ski in the Paralympics often use a special piece of equipment called a monoski. It has a seat fixed to one small ski. The skier uses two special poles called outriggers to help with balance.

Monoskis are sometimes called sit-skis.

outriggers

Athlete profile: Verena Bentele

Sport:	Biathlon and cross-country skiing
Country:	Germany
Olympic medals:	16, won at four different Paralympic Games, including five in the 2010 Games
Disability:	Verena is blind
Fact:	She won her first Paralympic medals at the age of 16

Verena Bentele and her guide winning the women's 3-kilometre biathlon at the 2010 Winter Paralympics

Short track speed skating became an Olympic event in 1992 after it became popular in the United States. In this sport, groups of four to six skaters start racing at the same time. Athletes need to be strong and skilful to move past each other to win the races.

22

Skaters put one hand down on the ice to balance on the tight corners.

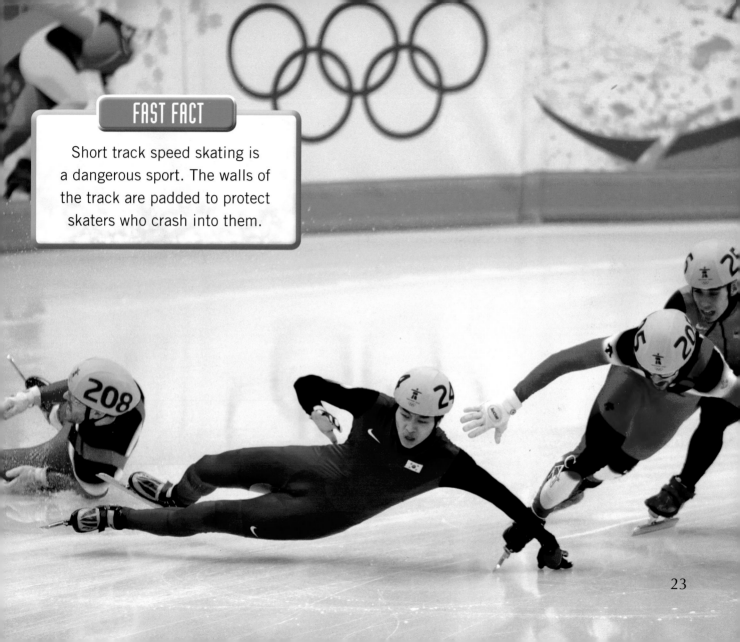

FAST FACT

Short track speed skating is
a dangerous sport. The walls of
the track are padded to protect
skaters who crash into them.

23

Snowboarding came into the Games in 1998 and is the newest sport in the Winter Olympics. It was developed in the United States in the 1980s and 1990s by young people who enjoyed surfing and skateboarding.

There are three different snowboarding events: parallel giant **slalom**, half-pipe and snowboard cross.

FAST FACT

The very first snowboards were made in the 1920s. Children tied wooden planks to their feet to slide down snowy hills!

24

Parallel giant slalom

Parallel giant slalom is a snowboard race where two competitors race each other side by side down a hill. They must **zig-zag** around a series of gates as they go.

Athlete profile: Jasey-Jay Anderson

Sport:	Snowboarding (slalom events)
Country:	Canada
Olympic medals:	Gold in 2010 men's parallel giant slalom
Fact:	Jasey-Jay started snowboarding at the age of 13

Half-pipe

In this event, snowboarders take off from a very steep wall of snow and do tricks in the air. Judges award points for each trick.

Judges watch for how well tricks are performed, how difficult they are, the height of jumps and good landings. They take off points for any mistakes.

Riders wear loose clothes to help them move and spin easily.

Snowboard cross

In the snowboard cross, competitors race against each other in groups. A special course is used which has tight turns and jumps. Racers need to be fearless and have great balance and **flexibility**.

There are often crashes in snowboard cross because the riders are so close together.

The Winter Olympics have grown hugely since they began in 1924. In the early days, most of the competitors were keen **amateurs** who played their sports for fun. Today, the athletes are often professionals who are paid to practise every day.

The Games will continue to grow and change. In the future, there may even be new sports to enjoy. Make sure you see the next Winter Olympics!

Glossary

amateurs	people who play sport for fun, not money
athletes	people who are very good at sport
competitors	people who take part in a sporting event
flexibility	being able to bend easily
human-made fabrics	materials which are not made from animals or plants
physical	to do with the body
plastic	human-made material that can be moulded into different shapes
puck	a disc made of hard rubber that is used in a hockey match
rifle	a type of gun
slalom	a ski race down a zig-zag course marked out by poles
style	the way something is done
zig-zag	turning sharply from left to right

The Winter Olympics timeline

ice hockey
in the Winter Olympics since 1924

ice skating
in the Winter Olympics since 1924

1924

1936

bobsleigh
in the Winter Olympics since 1924

downhill skiing
in the Winter Olympics since 1936

the Winter Paralympics
first took place in 1976

1976   1992   1998

short track speed skating
in the Winter Olympics since 1992

snowboarding
in the Winter Olympics since 1998

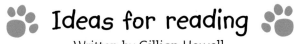

Ideas for reading

Written by Gillian Howell
Primary Literacy Consultant

Learning objectives: *(word reading objectives correspond with White band; all other objectives correspond with Copper band)* continue to apply phonic knowledge and skills as the route to decode words until automatic decoding has become embedded and reading is fluent; asking questions to improve their understanding of a text; identifying main ideas drawn from more than one paragraph and summarising these; retrieve and record information from non-fiction

Curriculum links: P.E.

Interest words: bobsleigh, Paralympics, competition, ceremony, skating, equipment, physical, protective, balance, original, dangerous, slalom

Word count: 1,300

Resources: pens, paper, art materials

Getting started

- Read the title together and look at the front cover. Ask the children to describe what they see in the photograph and what sport they think it is. Ask the children what they already know about the Olympics and the Winter Olympics and to suggest how the Winter Olympics differs from the Summer Olympics.

- Turn to the back cover and read the blurb. Ask the children to predict what sort of information they will find in this book, then read the contents page with the children to see if they were correct.

Reading and responding

- Ask the children to read the first two chapters aloud but in a quiet voice. Listen as they read and prompt as necessary. Remind them to use their phonic knowledge and the context to help them read words they are unsure of. Help the children with the pronunciation of *Chamonix* and *Vancouver.*

- Remind the children that information can also be found in the photographs and captions. On p3, ask the children to find out which countries have hosted the Winter Olympics and discuss why they may have been chosen, e.g. because they are cold countries.

- When the children have read the first two chapters, ask them to choose two more chapters from the list of contents, read them and make notes of facts and figures from their chosen chapters.